C000046287

RENOVATE
DECORATE
REINVIGORATE

*The beautifully simple planner for homeowners
who like a job done properly*

Susan Francombe

DEDICATION

To all those valiantly doing battle with paint, paper, curtains and flooring.
May your property nightmares turn into home sweet home.

And to Diana, for letting me take 12 months to finish painting the kitchen ceiling.

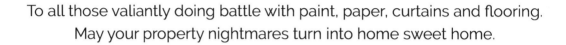

"Home is the nicest word there is." - Laura Ingalls Waller

CONTENTS

About The Author

Susan Francombe is a Chartered Civil Engineer and Barrister who has spent over 30 years working in the construction industry. She has spent much of that time dealing with the disputes that arise when things go wrong.

Realising that many homeowners and builders were getting into unnecessary arguments, she felt that there had to be a better way. Susan set up The Business Of Building to help people build better.

This planner is the first of a series of products aimed specifically at making life easier for homeowners. Giving them the knowledge and skills to get their projects completed on time, on budget and with less stress. Let Susan help you to take back control of your building and renovation projects.

Life is too short to waste on arguments, when you can do something more fun instead. Susan can be found in her free time whizzing around on a sexy Italian motorbike.

Website: www.businessofbuilding.co.uk
Facebook: @BIYHelp
Instagram: business-of-building
Pinterest: Business of Building
Email: susan@businessofbuilding.co.uk

Introduction

"Help – I don't know where to start?"

"There's too much choice.....how do I decide?"

"Can I afford to do it all?"

I've seen so many cries for help like those above from people starting to renovate their homes. That's why I decided to help by putting this planner together to make their lives easier.

What makes this planner special is that I have applied the lessons I've learned from my years working in the construction industry. Whether it's additional costs, extra delays or even just increased stress levels, these can be reduced or even prevented by better planning at the start. So, let me help you get the home renovation that you have dreamed of.

A clear concise and helpful planner for homeowners who don't know where to start

If this is you, don't panic. This planner will guide you through the basics in a clear concise and helpful manner. Packed with tips and useful pages to record your choices as you go along, you will find all you need to start your renovation journey. Covering everything from design styles and ideas, budgeting, time, planning and drawing out your ideas it also includes space to record everything in handy templates.

Know what you're doing? Here's a perfect planner to help you take control of your project

Not only does this planner record your ideas and purchases, it includes space to record and control your budget, detail your preparation and materials costs and record details of trades used. Storing all your decisions in one place.

Just to be clear, this planner deals with general renovation and redecoration works. If you are planning on having building work done such as extensions or loft conversions, it will help you design the interior. If you want great advice and tips on the building work itself then I cover this elsewhere both on my website and social media. Feel free to contact me – details are on page 4 – about the author

How to use this planner

Welcome to the start of your journey to Renovate, Decorate and Reinvigorate your home.

In this planner you will find sections to help you plan and control your budget, work out your timescale, outline your design ideas, record your decorating decisions, sketch your rooms, list your fixtures, fittings and furnishings, make a shopping list and keep track of trades quotes and costs.

Feel free to use the planner as you wish, but I suggest the following order.

1. Start by looking at the **Budget section**. This will help you set your overall cost target and explain how to keep your room renovation costs on track.

2. Head to the **Time section**. This helps you think about your overall timescale and gives you a practical way to estimate how long each room will take.

3. Do you know what styles you like? Have a look at the **Design Styles & Ideas section**, you might get some fresh inspiration.

4. The **Plans & Drawings section** will let you sketch out your room layouts and ideas.

5. Read the **Hints & Tips section** for things you might not have thought of.

6. Pick the rooms you are tackling and for each one fill out the planner pages. You'll find the following parts:

- Questions
- Keep/remove/replace/add checklist
- Plans & Drawings
- Buying List
- Budget
- Time
- Notes

If you need more pages for a particular room there are plenty more at the back of the planner in the **Spare Pages section**.

Finally, good luck and enjoy it!

Budget

It is so easy to get all excited and start work on renovating your home, only to end up with half-finished rooms and no more money. That's why you need to think about your budget. And yes, it can be the boring bit, but this planner will try and make it less of a chore.

Let's start with your overall budget for your home. How much money do you have to spend on everything? You need to stick to this – no secretly adding on extras on your credit card.

_____

_____

_____

_____

_____

_____

_____

Think about any trades that you are wanting to use. How much of the work are you doing yourself? Will you be hiring a decorator, plumber, electrician? If so, jot down their details here. Make sure you have their name, address and phone number.

_____

_____

_____

_____

_____

_____

_____

Budget

The budget section for each room is laid out as follows:

a) Room Budget – how much do you plan to spend on this room? How much did you actually spend?

b) Preparation Costs – if you are decorating the room yourself, there will be certain things you need to buy in order to prepare the room, such as sandpaper, masking tape and groundsheets. Don't forget safety equipment such as dust masks and safety glasses. You might also need to hire things such as floor sanders and wallpaper strippers.

c) Material Costs – make a list of all the materials you will need such as paint, wallpaper, skirting boards, tiles etc. When measuring don't forget you will need to add on extra. Things will need to be cut and trimmed, and allowances made for mistakes.

If materials are produced in batches, such as tiles or wallpaper, make sure you buy enough spare materials from the same batch. If you have to use a different batch the colours may not match up well. Most manufacturers usually give you guidance on wastage, particularly for wallpaper.

In general I suggest adding on an extra 20% to the order if you're unsure.

d) Buying List Costs – make a list of all the new items you are buying for the room. Whether it's a new chair, sofa, carpet, tv etc. Use the keep/remove/replace/add checklist to help you.

e) Trades Costs – if you are using trades to carry out works such as decorating, plastering etc put in their details, a description of the works and the quotation details.

Overall Room Costs – finally add up all the sections to get your overall room costs.

As you complete each room renovation, have a look at the actual cost compared to the estimated budget. You should be able to narrow down the cause of any difference.

Budget

Room	Estimated Budget	Final Costs
Total		

Budget

What are you over or under-estimating on your costs?

_____

_____

_____

_____

_____

_____

_____

How can you improve your forecasting for other rooms?

_____

_____

_____

_____

_____

_____

_____

Budget

If the estimated or actual costs are running too high for your overall budget, how do you prioritise?

I'm assuming that you are renovating your home to live in, rather than as an investment property. And that if needs be, you are happy to renovate over a period of time, putting up with some rooms as they are for a while.

Here's one suggestion.

1. Write a list of all the rooms you want to renovate.

2. Give each room a score of 1, 2 or 3 depending on how important they are to you. For example, think about how often you use them. Score 1 for not really important, 2 for neutral and 3 for really important. So, if you cook regularly you might score the kitchen a 3. If you just exist on takeaways, then you might score it a 1.

3. Give each room a score of 1, 2 or 3 depending on how much you love or hate them at the moment. 1 for love it or happy to keep it as it is for a while, 2 for neutral and 3 for hate it. Can you live with the bathroom for a while or are those tiles driving you mad!

4. Add up the scores for each room and start with the rooms with the highest score.

5. If you have a few rooms on the same score and your budget won't stretch to them all, then why not start with the rooms that are cheapest or quickest to do? You will feel like you've achieved more.

Here's an example:

IMPORTANCE:	LOVE/HATE
1 – Not really important	1 – Love it or happy to keep it as it is for a while
2 – Neutral	2 – Neutral
3 – Really important	3 – Hate it

Budget

Room	Importance	Love/hate	Total Score	Estimated cost
Kitchen	3	3	6	£5,000
Bathroom	2	3	5	£3,000
Living Room	2	2	4	£750
Bedroon	1	2	3	£1,000
Home Office /Study	3	1	4	£750
		Total Estimated Cost		£10,500
		Total Money Available		£6,000

As you can see, I haven't got enough money at the moment to renovate the whole house. Where do I start?

In this case the first room I would tackle would be the kitchen, as it has the highest total score (6). Basically, I hate it and it's really important to me! But that takes a chunk of my renovation budget. As I've only £1,000 left I can't afford to tackle the bathroom which has the next highest total score (5). I can wait until I have saved up the extra £2,000. Or if I want to carry on renovating now I can choose between the home office/study and living room. Both have the same total score (4) and can be completed for less than £1,000 each.

Budget

Here's a blank one for you to use:

Room	Importance	Love/hate	Total Score	Estimated cost
Total Estimated Cost				
Total Money Available				

NOTES

NOTES

Time

You might be lucky and have all the time in the world to complete your renovation. Or you might have a deadline, such as a new child arriving or a big family get together that you want to be ready for.

Do you have a deadline for completing your renovation? What is it?

_____

_____

_____

_____

_____

For each room you are renovating, you are going to estimate the time it will take to complete. I'll give you an example of how you might do this using the Time chart.

Start by listing all the things that you can think of you need to do to complete the room renovation. This might include stripping wallpaper, buying new flooring, painting woodwork, putting together flat pack cupboards etc. List them all out in the items section.

Now try and sort out a logical flow for the things you need to do. Think about the potential mess and damage that each step might cause. If your room needs rewiring that's best to get done first. If your ceiling needs to be plastered, it would make sense to have that done before you have the walls and floor finished (plastering can be messy!). Use the Time chart to list all the items down in the order that makes most sense.

Try and estimate how long each item will take to complete. Be realistic. You won't be able to sand down all the walls and paint them with two coats in a single day. Allow yourself some down time. If you are employing trades make sure you get a start date and end date from them. Add on a bit of extra time for delays.

Finally make a note of any key dates. When will the plasterer start work? Will it take two weeks for your new cupboards to be delivered?

Time

Timing issues

Item	Estimated Time	Key Dates	Notes
Order new cupboards	2 weeks delivery		Ordered 15th May
New flooring			Already bought
Remove contents of room	1/2 Day		
Strip wallpaper	1 Day		
Plasterer	3 Days	Sat 3rd June	
Clean and prepare walls	2 Days		
Clean and prepare woodwork	1 Day		
Paint ceiling	3 Days		3 coats
Paint walls	2 Days		2 coats
Paint woodwork	2 Days		2 coats
Put together cupboards	1/2 Day		
Fit cupboards	1/2 Day		
Lay new flooring	4 Days		
Change socket covers	1/4 Day		
Change door handle	1/4 Day		

So, I know it will take me roughly 17 days to complete the work, and the plasterer will take 3 days to finish his work. If my deadline for completing the room is 1 July, then that should be achievable.

NOTES

NOTES

Design Styles & Ideas

Planning a renovation can be overwhelming – too many styles, too many choices. So, use these pages to narrow down how you want your home to look and feel.

Overall Style

Interior designers use a whole range of names to describe the different styles you can use to furnish a room. Here's my take on some of the styles you might want to consider. Use the checklist on the following page to mark up your favourites, cross off the ones that are definitely not you, add any other ones that you like. These could even be the names of designers or shops whose style you like. Jot down your thoughts and inspirations in the notes.

Traditional	Wooden panels, picture rails, thick curtains and pelmets, display cabinets, paintings, formal dining tables, dark wood, heavy ornate furniture, Chesterfield sofas, wingback chairs, fireplaces, patterned wallpaper, floral patterned furnishings. Think stately home on a smaller scale.
Modern / Contemporary	Clean crisp lines, simple colour schemes but with the occasional bright colours, plain furniture, materials such as glass and metal, open-plan, no clutter or fuss but maybe the occasional quirky item.
Scandinavian	Simple, clean, natural textures, wood panelling, wood flooring, light wood furniture, uncluttered.
Eclectic	A posh word for a bit of everything! Will have elements from a number of different styles. If you have travelled abroad, then why not show off items you have collected on your travels.
Minimalist	Functional furniture, clean crisp lines, simple design, only essential items in the room, little decoration. Hide everything!
Rococo	Highly decorated furniture, with elaborate carvings, gold decorations, cherubs, angels, flowers. Large wall paintings. Go over the top.
Bohemian	You could be looking at different tribal and ethnic styles, drapes, wall hangings, rugs, throws, maybe in mismatched bright colours. Different types of furniture can be mixed together.

Design Styles & Ideas

Farmhouse	Ceiling beams, stone walls, wooden or tile flooring, open shelving, wooden cabinets and furniture, warm colours, rugs, pots and pans on display, farmhouse sinks, range style cookers.
Beach House / Coastal	Light colours, mainly whites, blues and greens, wooden furniture, ocean themed pictures and ornaments, stripes. Think Blackpool or Miami, depending on your style!
Glamour/ Glitz	Bold designs and colours, large mirrors, jewels, gold decorations, neon, fake furs. Anything that shouts at you.
Industrial	Imagine a warehouse or industrial building, raw walls, exposed brick, pipes and steelwork, unfinished look, open-plan, re-used materials.
Mediterranean	Think of Greek or Spanish holidays – tile and brick flooring, stone or white walls, bold colours as decoration.
Art Deco	A style from the 1920s/1930s. Glitzy, with geometric designs, mirrors, bold prints & wallpaper. Metallic finishes and dark colours.
Zen	Clean lines, simplicity in design, red, gold and black objects such as prints or vases, dragons, birds and flower decorations, natural wood.
Shabby chic	Into DIY and crafting? Distressed furnishings, upscaled old furniture, vintage reimagined, patterned prints, wall hangings, plants.

Design Styles & Ideas

Overall Style Checklist

	YES	MAYBE	NO	Notes
Traditional			✓	
Modern/ Contemporary				
Scandinavian				
Eclectic				
Minimalist				
Rococo				
Bohemian				
Farmhouse			✓	
Beach House/ Coastal			✓	
Glamour / Glitz				
Industrial			✓	
Mediterranean				
Art Deco				
Zen				
Shabby Chic				

Notes

Notes

Flooring

Are you a wooden floors and rugs person, or do you love thick fluffy carpets? Let's list some of the types of flooring you can choose.

Hardwood	Solid wood flooring – everything from oak, walnut and cherry to lighter coloured woods such as pine.
Engineered Wood	A laminate with real wood on top and plywood underneath.
Bamboo	Becoming more popular as an alternative to hardwood flooring.
Floorboards	Sanded and varnished or painted.
Laminate	A variety of finishes, so the choice is huge. Comes in various colours and textures and can be made to look like wood or tiles.
Vinyl	Mainly available as sheets or tiles. Again, a whole range of different designs is available. Different colour tiles can be arranged to make your own patterns.
Carpet / Rugs	So many different types, short-pile for busy rooms, long-pile luxury for bedrooms. Lots of colours and styles.
Lino	Mainly available as sheets or tiles.
Cork	Most common as tiles, can help with soundproofing.
Tiles	There are many different types of floor tiles, such as terracotta, quarry, porcelain and ceramic.
Concrete	Poured and polished concrete floors can look good in a modern house.
Stone	Lots of choices available, including slate, marble, travertine and limestone.

Flooring Checklist

	YES	MAYBE	NO	Notes
Hardwood				
Engineered Wood				
Bamboo				
Floorboards				
Laminate				
Vinyl				
Carpet / Rugs				
Lino				
Cork				
Tiles				
Concrete				
Stone				

Notes

Notes

Window Treatments

There's more to windows than just curtains. Here's a few suggestions, but don't forget you can leave windows bare if you want!

Curtains	Fabric that hangs just below the window sill.
Drapes	Normally heavier fabric than curtains, hangs down to the floor.
Roller Blinds	Fabric that unrolls using a chain and can go either inside or outside of the window frame.
Roll-up Blinds	Similar to roller blinds but you roll up the material yourself and tie-it in position.
Roman Blinds	Pleated material that raises and lowers in sections.
Venetian / Slatted Blinds	Horizontal blinds made out of vinyl or wood that pivot open and shut.
Vertical Slatted Blinds	Vertical blinds made out of fabric that are attached to a top sliding track.
Bamboo / Rattan Blinds	Similar to roller blinds but made out of bamboo or woven wood.
Shutters	Wooden or PVC shutters can either be solid or slatted.
Sheer Panels / Voile / Lace	These don't stop light coming but can be used for privacy.
Pelmet	A decorative board that goes above the window to hide the curtain fixings and rail.
Window Films	Plain, patterned or coloured films stuck onto the glass for privacy or to prevent fading.

Window Checklist

	YES	MAYBE	NO	Notes
Curtains				
Drapes				
Roller Blinds				
Roll-up Blinds				
Roman Blinds				
Venetian / Slatted Blinds				
Vertical Slatted Blinds				
Bamboo / Rattan Blinds				
Shutters				
Sheer Panels / Voile / Lace				
Pelmet				
Window Films				

Notes

Notes

Plans & Drawings

It's always useful to have a floor plan to help you decide on your room layout

Use the following pages to draw out your rooms as they are now, and then how you want them to look afterwards.

Don't forget to add measurements! These are important when you start adding furniture to a room. I've seen a living room where you couldn't shut the door as the sofa was too long!

Elevation drawings are also useful. An elevation is just a picture of the walls as you look at them.

I've included an example room to show you how to mark up the details you need. As you can see, you don't need to be a great artist – I'm not!

There are two pages of empty planning sheets here, two pages for each room and extra pages at the back of the planner. There are scales on the pages to help you with your drawings. Pick whichever scale best fits the size of your room. Or use your own scale if you feel confident.

If you really want to be sure that things will fit, mark out the actual size of the item on the floor in masking tape. When designing our kitchen we marked out the size of the island we had planned to make sure that we still had plenty of room to walk around.

I know many people struggle to understand plans and drawings though, so don't be afraid if this is you. There are some great online programs and apps that simply take your measurements and turn them into 3-d rooms. Some measure the room for you using your camera and some others even allow you to produce walk-through videos. What is available changes all the time, but as at the end of 2020 some of the free or relatively cheap ones you can use are SketchUp, Floorplanner and Roomstyler 3D Home Planner. But have a look in your app store.

Plans & Drawings

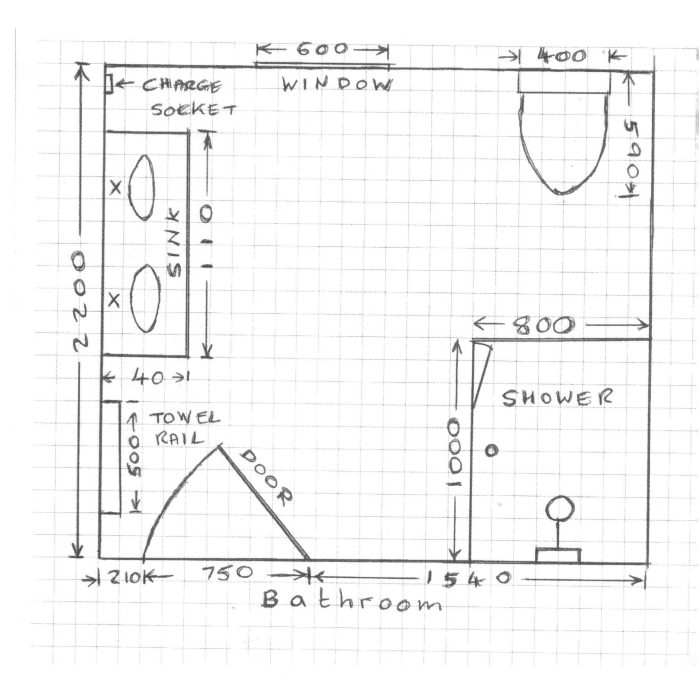

Plans & Drawings

Room:

Plans & Drawings

Room:

Metres

1   2   3   4   5

1   2   3   4   5

Hints & tips

Now that you know what style you like, it's time to turn to designing the rooms of your home. I'm not a mind reader and don't know the layout of your house. So I have set out pages for one each of the common room types you might have, and then left blank templates in the Spare Pages section of this planner.

So, whether you are starting small, with a 1-bedroom flat, or going large with a 5-bedroom house with 5 bathrooms, a spa and a cinema, you'll find this planner helpful.

Before heading to each room, there are a couple of other things to consider.

Storage

Work out how much you need and add extra. We always need more storage than we think. Are there any wasted spaces you could use? Do you have loft space that could be boarded out? Why not use your renovation works as an excuse to have a clear out?

Lighting

There are loads of options when it comes to lighting. LED ceiling lights, chandeliers, wall lights, standard lamps, spotlights, undercounter lighting, floor lights, uplighters, downlighters...

Think about how you are going to use the space. During the day you might want to arrange your chair or desk so that you get as much natural light as possible. How will that light get in? Can you change this using different colours or surface finishes?

Do you want to stop light getting in? If you work nights, you want to be able to sleep during the day. If you are watching tv you don't want the sun shining in your eyes or on your screen.

Do you want to be able to dim the lights, or make them change colour remotely? (I like setting our kitchen lights to change colour in time to the music I play when cooking).

There are lots of different options - let your imagination run wild. You could even use light boxes and fibre optics to have the galaxy projected on your ceiling.

Sockets / plugs

Don't leave it until the last minute to realise that you've only got one plug socket in the living room and it is the opposite side of the room to where you want your standard lamp plugged in. Always put in more than you think you will need.

If you need electrical work carried out, get this done before you start decorating. And make sure you use a qualified electrician.

Hints & Tips

Smart Homes/Technology

Most people are now using technology every day at home. Whether it's an online chat to family or friends or giving a business presentation on Zoom wearing your best shirt and your pyjama bottoms.

Our equipment is also talking to our homes, with wi-fi fridges, washing machines and even toothbrushes connect to the internet. Think about where your routers and electrical equipment can go. Do you need any boosters to reach particular rooms? Or would you be better off having a wired system installed?

Many people are also adding in security systems – do you want sensors, cameras, smoke alarms etc that are all connected and controlled by apps?

Employing Decorators, Electricians, Kitchen Fitters etc.

If you are employing others to do part of the work, PLEASE PLEASE PLEASE sort out your contract. It doesn't have to be difficult or complex. You can even refuse to call it a contract if you'd prefer. It's just a record of what you have agreed.

Just make sure you are clear on exactly what the trader is to do, what materials they are to supply, how much they are going to charge, when they are to be paid, and how long they have to complete the works. Get it in writing – text messages, emails, written quotes are fine.

If you want help with this I have produced a really simple agreement and guide that is available from www.businessofbuilding.co.uk.

Mood Boards

A mood board is somewhere to collect pictures and images of things you like. You can start a physical scrapbook to cut out and keep furniture ideas from magazines and brochures; material samples or paint swatches. Or start an online mood board using apps and programs such as Trello, Canva and Pinterest. Either way, gathering images together is a great way of getting a feel for the colours and style of your renovation.

Notes

Notes

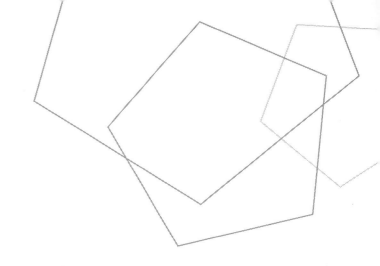

HALLWAY / ENTRANCE

Hallway/Entrance

The questions

The first room you see when you walk into your home. Why not try and make it warm and inviting? Or give it the wow factor?

What do you like about the room as it is?

_____

_____

_____

_____

_____

What don't you like about the room as it is?

_____

_____

_____

_____

_____

How do you want to use it? Will it be for passing through only, for waiting in, for storing wet coats and umbrellas? How do you want it to feel – warm, cosy, practical?

_____

_____

_____

_____

_____

Hallway/Entrance

What design style are you going for in this room?

What colours are you going to use?

Are there any must haves in your hallway/entrance? A table, a mirror, a shoe rack...? Jot them down here.

Hallway/Entrance

What sort of lighting do you want to have? LED ceiling lights, wall lights, uplighters, downlighters?

Where are all the electrical sockets? Do they need to be moved? Do you want to change the covers?

What do you want to do to the walls & ceilings? Paper, paint, add texture, cladding, coving?

Hallway/Entrance

The keep/remove/replace/add checklist

	Keep	Remove	Replace	Add	Notes
Flooring					
Doors / Handles					
Walls					
Ceiling					
Window Covering					
Lighting					
Doorbell/Video					
Table					
Shoerack					
Key/Mail Storage					
Mirror					
Rug					
Coatrack					
Chair					
Umbrella Storage					
Pictures/Art					
Skirting Boards					

Hallway/Entrance

The keep/remove/replace/add checklist

	Keep	Remove	Replace	Add	Notes
Sockets					
Radiators					

Hallway/Entrance

Plans & Drawings:

Metres

1 2 3 4 5

1 2 3 4 5

47

Hallway/Entrance

Plans & Drawings:

Metres

Hallway/Entrance

Buying list

Type:	Shop / Website
Description	
Cost	

Type:	Shop / Website
Description	
Cost	

Type:	Shop / Website
Description	
Cost	

Hallway/Entrance

Buying list

Type:	Shop / Website
Description	
Cost	

Type:	Shop / Website
Description	
Cost	

Type:	Shop / Website
Description	
Cost	

Hallway/Entrance

Buying list

Type:	Shop / Website
Description	
Cost	

Type:	Shop / Website
Description	
Cost	

Type:	Shop / Website
Description	
Cost	

Hallway/Entrance

Buying list

Type:	Shop / Website
Description	
Cost	

Type:	Shop / Website
Description	
Cost	

Type:	Shop / Website
Description	
Cost	

Total Buying Cost for Room:

Hallway/Entrance

Budget

a) Room Budget

Item	Estimated Cost	Actual Cost
Preparation Costs		
Material Costs		
Buying List Costs		
Trades Costs		
Total		

b) Preparation Costs

Item	Estimated Cost	Actual Cost
Total		

Hallway/Entrance

Budget

c) Material Costs

Item	Estimated Cost	Actual Cost
Total		

d) Total Buying List Costs

Item	Estimated Cost	Actual Cost
Total		

Hallway/Entrance

Budget

e) Trades Cost

Type:	Trader's Name
Description of works	
Quoted Cost	

Type:	Trader's Name
Description of works	
Quoted Cost	

Type:	Trader's Name
Description of works	
Quoted Cost	

Total Buying List Costs for Room:

Hallway/Entrance

Time

Item	Estimated time	Key dates	Notes

Notes

Notes

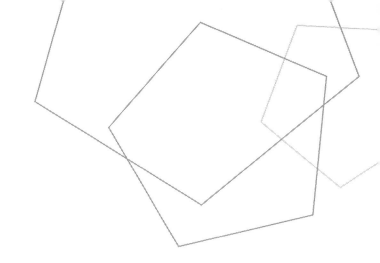

LIVING
ROOM

Living Room

The questions

The room you relax in after finishing work. The room you share when friends come to visit. What do you want it to say about you? What will make you feel relaxed and at home?

What do you like about the room as it is?

What don't you like about the room as it is?

How do you want to use it? Do you want reclining seats to put your feet up? Would you prefer a large tv or a fire or picture as the focal point of the room? How do you want it to feel – warm, cosy, practical?

Living Room

What design style are you going for in this room?

_____

_____

_____

_____

_____

What colours are you going to use?

_____

_____

_____

_____

_____

Are there any must haves in your living room? Reclining chairs, coffee table, media stand...? Jot them down here.

_____

_____

_____

_____

Living Room

What sort of lighting do you want to have? LED ceiling lights, wall lights, uplighters, downlighters?

_____

_____

_____

_____

_____

Where are all the electrical sockets? Do they need to be moved? Do you want to change the covers?

_____

_____

_____

_____

_____

What do you want to do to the walls and ceilings? Paper, paint, add texture, cladding, coving?

_____

_____

_____

_____

_____

Living Room

The keep/remove/replace/add checklist

	Keep	Remove	Replace	Add	Notes
Flooring					
Doors / Handles					
Walls					
Ceiling					
Window Covering					
Lighting					
Sofa					
Coffee Table					
Media Stand					
Side Table					
Chair					
Rug					
Cushions					
Throw					
Pictures / Art					
Skirting Boards					

Living Room

The keep/remove/replace/add checklist

	Keep	Remove	Replace	Add	Notes
Sockets					
TV / Media Centre					
Sound System					
Radiators					

Living Room

Plans & Drawings

Metres

1   2   3   4   5

1 2 3 4 5

Living Room

Plans & drawings

Metres

Living Room

Buying list

Type:	Shop / Website
Description	
Cost	

Type:	Shop / Website
Description	
Cost	

Type:	Shop / Website
Description	
Cost	

Living Room
Buying list

Type:	Shop / Website
Description	
Cost	

Type:	Shop / Website
Description	
Cost	

Type:	Shop / Website
Description	
Cost	

Living Room

Buying list

Type:	Shop / Website
Description	
Cost	

Type:	Shop / Website
Description	
Cost	

Type:	Shop / Website
Description	
Cost	

Living Room

Buying list

Type:	Shop / Website
Description	
Cost	

Type:	Shop / Website
Description	
Cost	

Type:	Shop / Website
Description	
Cost	

Total Buying List Costs for Room:

Living Room
Budget

a) Room Budget

Item	Estimated Cost	Actual Cost
Preparation Costs		
Material Costs		
Buying List Costs		
Trades Costs		
Total		

b) Preparation Costs

Item	Estimated Cost	Actual Cost
Total		

Living Room
Budget

c) Material Costs

Item	Estimated Cost	Actual Cost
Total		

d) Total Buying List Costs

Item	Estimated Cost	Actual Cost
Total		

Living Room

Budget

e) Trades Cost

Type:	Trader's Name
Description of works:	
Quoted Cost:	**Final Cost:**

Type:	Trader's Name
Description of works:	
Quoted Cost:	**Final Cost:**

Type:	Trader's Name
Description of works:	
Quoted Cost:	**Final Cost:**

Total Trades Costs:

Overall Room Costs:

Living Room

Time

Item	Estimated time	Key dates	Notes

Notes

Notes

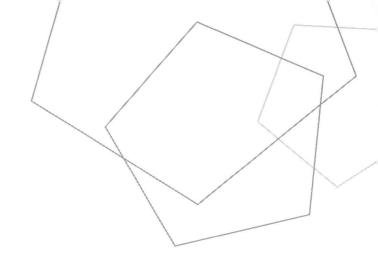

KITCHEN

Kitchen

The questions

From a small compact kitchen to a large party room, from somewhere you just burn the toast to somewhere you prepare meals worthy of a celebrity chef. What sort of kitchen will you design?

What do you like about the room as it is?

_____

_____

_____

_____

_____

What don't you like about the room as it is?

_____

_____

_____

_____

_____

How do you want to use it? Will it be adults only, family with young children, a working space or a chilled, don't worry about the mess space? How do you want it to feel – warm, cosy, practical?

_____

_____

_____

_____

_____

Kitchen

What design style are you going for in this room?

_____

_____

_____

_____

What colours are you going to use?

_____

_____

_____

_____

Are there any must haves in your kitchen? An island, a hot tap, an overhead extractor, a microwave...? Jot them down here.

_____

_____

_____

_____

Kitchen

What sort of lighting do you want to have? LED ceiling lights, spotlamps, wall lights, lights under wall cabinets?

Where are all the electrical sockets? Do they need to be moved?

What do you want to do to the walls and ceilings? Paper, paint, add texture, cladding, coving?

Kitchen

The keep/remove/replace/add checklist

	Keep	Remove	Replace	Add	Notes
Flooring					
Doors / Handles					
Walls					
Ceiling					
Window Covering					
Lighting					
Cooker					
Oven					
Microwave					
Worktops					
Cupboards					
Extractor Fan					
Sinks					
Tiles					
Splashback					
Fridge					

Kitchen

The keep/remove/replace/add checklist

	Keep	Remove	Replace	Add	Notes
Freezer					
Dishwasher					
Washing Machine					
Dryer					
Sockets					
Range Cooker					
Radiators					
Skirting Boards					

Kitchen

Plans & Drawings

Metres

1 2 3 4 5

1 2 3 4 5

Kitchen

Plans & Drawings

Metres

1 2 3 4 5

1 2 3 4 5

Kitchen

Buying list

Type:	Shop / Website
Description	
Cost	

Type:	Shop / Website
Description	
Cost	

Type:	Shop / Website
Description	
Cost	

Kitchen

Buying list

Type:	Shop / Website
Description	
Cost	

Type:	Shop / Website
Description	
Cost	

Type:	Shop / Website
Description	
Cost	

Kitchen

Buying list

Type:	Shop / Website
Description	
Cost	

Type:	Shop / Website
Description	
Cost	

Type:	Shop / Website
Description	
Cost	

Kitchen

Buying list

Type:	Shop / Website
Description	
Cost	

Type:	Shop / Website
Description	
Cost	

Type:	Shop / Website
Description	
Cost	

Total Buying List Costs for Room:

Kitchen

Budget

a) Room Budget

Item	Estimated Cost	Actual Cost
Preparation Costs		
Material Costs		
Buying List Costs		
Trades Costs		
Total		

b) Preparation Costs

Item	Estimated Cost	Actual Cost
Total		

Kitchen
Budget

c) Material Costs

Item	Estimated Cost	Actual Cost
Total		

d) Total Buying List Costs

Item	Estimated Cost	Actual Cost
Total		

Kitchen

Budget

e) Trades Cost

Type:	Trader's Name
Description of works:	
Quoted Cost:	**Final Cost:**

Type:	Trader's Name
Description of works:	
Quoted Cost:	**Final Cost:**

Type:	Trader's Name
Description of works:	
Quoted Cost:	**Final Cost:**

Total Trades Costs:

Overall Room Costs:

Kitchen

Time

Item	Estimated time	Key dates	Notes

Notes

Notes

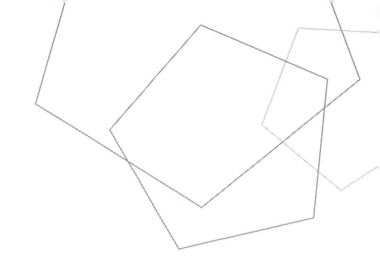

UTILITY ROOM

Utility Room

The questions

Some houses have a separate utility room for things like the washing machines, storage etc. If you are renovating yours, there's still plenty of things to think about. Can you improve your storage? Have you got worktop space to sort out your washing?

You can also consider using the utility room for other things. Do you want to store some of your kitchen items here, such as tinned food? Do you have dogs that need storage for their toys, leads etc? Or even a space for them to stay if they're wet after a walk until they dry off?

You might even want to use to utility room to store sports equipment. Are there places on the walls where they can be hung from or stored?

If you are turning a room into a utility room, don't forget to think about the plumbing - where can your washing machine, sink etc plug into the water and drainage?

What do you like about the room as it is?

_____

_____

_____

_____

What don't you like about the room as it is?

_____

_____

_____

_____

How do you want to use it? Do you want to iron in it, fold laundry, store your children's/dogs/sports things? How do you want it to feel – warm, cosy, practical?

_____

_____

_____

_____

Utility Room

What design style are you going for in this room?

_____

_____

_____

_____

_____

What colours are you going to use?

_____

_____

_____

_____

_____

Are there any must haves in your utility room? Space for ironing, shoe and coat racks...? Jot them down here.

_____

_____

_____

_____

_____

Utility Room

What sort of lighting do you want to have? LED ceiling lights, spotlamps, wall lights, lights under wall cabinets?

_____

_____

_____

_____

_____

Where are all the electrical sockets? Do they need to be moved? Do you want to change the covers?

_____

_____

_____

_____

_____

What do you want to do to the walls and ceilings? Paper, paint, add texture, cladding, coving?

_____

_____

_____

_____

_____

Utility Room

The keep/remove/replace/add checklist

	Keep	Remove	Replace	Add	Notes
Flooring					
Doors / Handles					
Walls					
Ceiling					
Window Covering					
Lighting					
Worktops					
Cupboards					
Sinks					
Tiles					
Splashback					
Dishwasher					
Washing Machine					
Dryer					
Sockets					
Shoe Rack					

Utility Room

The keep/remove/replace/add checklist

	Keep	Remove	Replace	Add	Notes
Pet Washing Area					
Ironing Area					
Radiators					
Skirting Boards					

Utility Room

Plans & Drawings

Metres

Utility Room

Plans & Drawings

Metres

Utility Room

Buying list

Type:	Shop / Website
Description	
Cost	

Type:	Shop / Website
Description	
Cost	

Type:	Shop / Website
Description	
Cost	

Utility Room

Buying list

Type:	Shop / Website
Description	
Cost	

Type:	Shop / Website
Description	
Cost	

Type:	Shop / Website
Description	
Cost	

Utility Room

Buying list

Type:	Shop / Website
Description	
Cost	

Type:	Shop / Website
Description	
Cost	

Type:	Shop / Website
Description	
Cost	

Utility Room

Buying list

Type:	Shop / Website
Description	
Cost	

Type:	Shop / Website
Description	
Cost	

Type:	Shop / Website
Description	
Cost	

Total Buying List Cost for Room:

Utility Room
Budget

a) Room Budget

Item	Estimated Cost	Actual Cost
Preparation Costs		
Material Costs		
Buying List Costs		
Trades Costs		
Total		

b) Preparation Costs

Item	Estimated Cost	Actual Cost
Total		

Utility Room

Budget

c) Material Costs

Item	Estimated Cost	Actual Cost
Total		

d) Total Buying List Costs

Item	Estimated Cost	Actual Cost
Total		

Utility Room

Budget

e) Trades Cost

Type:	Trader's Name
Description of works:	
Quoted Cost:	**Final Cost:**

Type:	Trader's Name
Description of works:	
Quoted Cost:	**Final Cost:**

Type:	Trader's Name
Description of works:	
Quoted Cost:	**Final Cost:**

Total Trades Costs:

Overall Room Costs:

Utility Room

Time

Item	Estimated time	Key dates	Notes

Notes

Notes

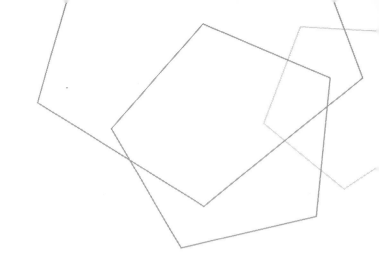

BATHROOM/
SHOWER ROOM

Bathroom/Shower Room

The questions

For some a bathroom is a place to laze for hours reading a good book or catching up on the latest box set whilst sinking into the bubble bath. For others it's the joy of a long hot shower to set the day up right. Or it might be trying to get the kids washed and off to school without flooding the house!

However you plan to use your bathroom or shower room, let's get your plans written down here so you can be on your way to realising your dream.

What do you like about the room as it is?

_____

_____

_____

_____

_____

What don't you like about the room as it is?

_____

_____

_____

_____

_____

How do you want to use it? As a place to spend quality time in? Or a simply practical room? How do you want it to feel – warm, cosy, practical?

_____

_____

_____

_____

_____

Bathroom/Shower Room

What design style are you going for in this room?

_____

_____

_____

_____

What colours are you going to use?

_____

_____

_____

_____

Are there any must haves in your bathroom or shower room? Tiles, powerful shower, jet batch...? Jot them down here.

_____

_____

_____

_____

Bathroom/Shower Room

What sort of lighting do you want to have? LED ceiling lights, light-up mirror?

Do you need a socket to charge your toothbrush?

What do you want to do to the walls and ceilings? Paper, paint, add texture, cladding, coving?

Bathroom/Shower Room

The keep/remove/replace/add checklist

	Keep	Remove	Replace	Add	Notes
Flooring					
Doors					
Window Covering					
Lighting					
Bath					
Shower					
Shower Screen / Curtain					
Tiles					
Wall Panels					
Extractor Fan					
Sink					
Storage Unit					
Taps					
Towel Rail					
Toilet					
Charging Socket					

Bathroom/Shower Room

The keep/remove/replace/add checklist

	Keep	Remove	Replace	Add	Notes
Picture					
Mirror					
Toilet Brush					
Shower / Bath Caddy					
Bidet					
Radiators					
Skirting Boards					

Bathroom/Shower Room

Metres

Plans & Drawings

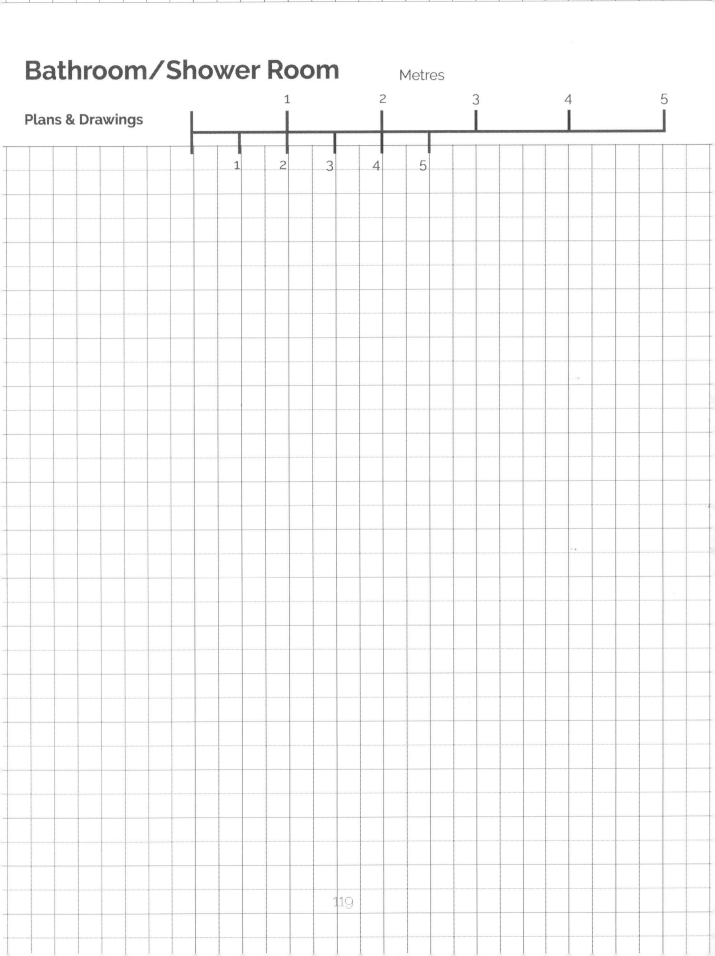

Bathroom/Shower Room

Plans & Drawings

Metres

1 2 3 4 5

1 2 3 4 5

Bathroom/Shower Room

Buying list

Type:	Shop / Website
Description	
Cost	

Type:	Shop / Website
Description	
Cost	

Type:	Shop / Website
Description	
Cost	

Bathroom/Shower Room

Buying list

Type:	Shop / Website
Description	
Cost	

Type:	Shop / Website
Description	
Cost	

Type:	Shop / Website
Description	
Cost	

Bathroom/Shower Room

Buying list

Type:	Shop / Website
Description	
Cost	

Type:	Shop / Website
Description	
Cost	

Type:	Shop / Website
Description	
Cost	

Bathroom/Shower Room

Buying list

Type:	Shop / Website
Description	
Cost	

Type:	Shop / Website
Description	
Cost	

Type:	Shop / Website
Description	
Cost	

Total Buying List Cost for Room:

Bathroom/Shower Room

Budget

a) Room Budget

Item	Estimated Cost	Actual Cost
Preparation Costs		
Material Costs		
Buying List Costs		
Trades Costs		
Total		

b) Preparation Costs

Item	Estimated Cost	Actual Cost
Total		

Bathroom/Shower Room
Budget

c) Material Costs

Item	Estimated Cost	Actual Cost
Total		

d) Total Buying List Costs

Item	Estimated Cost	Actual Cost
Total		

Bathroom/Shower Room

Budget

e) Trades Cost

Type:	Trader's Name
Description of works:	
Quoted Cost:	**Final Cost:**

Type:	Trader's Name
Description of works:	
Quoted Cost:	**Final Cost:**

Type:	Trader's Name
Description of works:	
Quoted Cost:	**Final Cost:**

Total Trades Costs:

Overall Room Costs:

Bathroom/Shower Room

Time

Item	Estimated time	Key dates	Notes

Notes

Notes

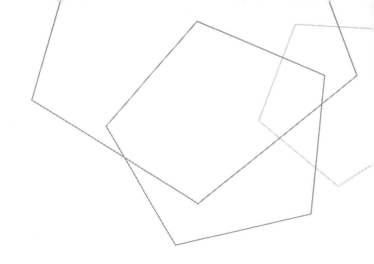

BEDROOM

Bedroom

Whether it's a master bedroom that you want to feel warm and cosy; a spare bedroom that will only occasionally be used or a children's bedroom that doubles as a play room, let's get it planned here.

What do you like about the room as it is?

What don't you like about the room as it is?

How do you want to use it? As a place to spend quality time in? Or a simply practical room? How do you want it to feel – warm, cosy, practical?

Bedroom

What design style are you going for in this room?

_____

_____

_____

_____

_____

What colours are you going to use?

_____

_____

_____

_____

_____

Are there any must haves in your bedroom? A fitted wardrobe, a TV, a chair...? Jot them down here.

_____

_____

_____

_____

_____

Bedroom

What sort of lighting do you want to have? LED ceiling lights, wall lights, bedside table lights?

_____

_____

_____

_____

Where are all the electrical sockets? Do they need to be moved? Do you want to replace the covers?

_____

_____

_____

_____

What do you want to do to the walls and ceilings? Paper, paint, add texture, cladding, coving?

_____

_____

_____

_____

Bedroom

The keep/remove/replace/add checklist

	Keep	Remove	Replace	Add	Notes
Flooring					
Doors / Handles					
Window Covering					
Lighting					
Bed					
Bedside Tables					
Chair					
Wardrobe					
Headboard					
Mirror					
Drawes					
TV					
Rug					
Pictures					
Throw					
Sockets					

Bedroom

The keep/remove/replace/add checklist

	Keep	Remove	Replace	Add	Notes
Mattress					
Bedding					
Cushions					
Radiators					
Skirting Boards					

Bedroom

Plans & Drawings

Metres

Bedroom

Plans & Drawings

Metres

Bedroom

Buying list

Type:	Shop / Website
Description	
Cost	

Type:	Shop / Website
Description	
Cost	

Type:	Shop / Website
Description	
Cost	

Bedroom

Buying list

Type:	Shop / Website
Description	
Cost	

Type:	Shop / Website
Description	
Cost	

Type:	Shop / Website
Description	
Cost	

Bedroom

Buying list

Type:	Shop / Website
Description	
Cost	

Type:	Shop / Website
Description	
Cost	

Type:	Shop / Website
Description	
Cost	

Bedroom

Budget

Type:	Shop / Website
Description	
Cost	

Type:	Shop / Website
Description	
Cost	

Type:	Shop / Website
Description	
Cost	

Total Buying Cost for Room:

Bedroom

Budget

a) Room Budget

Item	Estimated Cost	Actual Cost
Preparation Costs		
Material Costs		
Buying List Costs		
Trades Costs		
Total		

b) Preparation Costs

Item	Estimated Cost	Actual Cost
Total		

Bedroom
Budget

c) Material Costs

Item	Estimated Cost	Actual Cost
Total		

d) Total Buying List Costs

Item	Estimated Cost	Actual Cost
Total		

Bedroom

Budget

e) Trades Cost

Type:	Trader's Name
Description of works:	
Quoted Cost:	**Final Cost:**

Type:	Trader's Name
Description of works:	
Quoted Cost:	**Final Cost:**

Type:	Trader's Name
Description of works:	
Quoted Cost:	**Final Cost:**

Total Trades Costs:

Overall Room Costs:

Bedroom

Time

Item	Estimated time	Key dates	Notes

Notes

Notes

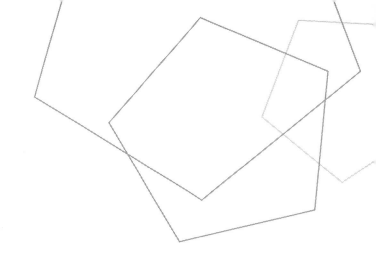

HOME OFFICE / STUDY

Home Office/Study

The questions

With more and more people working from home at least part of the time, why not turn a small room into a fully kitted office space?

Think about the IT that you will need. Make sure your incoming broadband supply is nearby and that you can get good wifi and telephone connections here.

Do you fancy a quirky style like the tech startups with table football and video games, or the more traditional wooden desk and bookshelves approach?

What do you like about the room as it is?

_____

_____

_____

_____

What don't you like about the room as it is?

_____

_____

_____

_____

How do you want to use it? Will you be inviting colleagues and clients to visit? How do you want it to feel – warm, cosy, practical?

_____

_____

_____

_____

Home Office/Study

What design style are you going for in this room?

_____

_____

_____

_____

What colours are you going to use?

_____

_____

_____

_____

Are there any must haves in your Home Office? Additional charging points, a TV, a visitor's chair...? Jot them down here.

_____

_____

_____

_____

Home Office/Study

What sort of lighting do you want to have? LED ceiling lights, wall lights, bedside table lights?

Where are all the electrical sockets? Do they need to be moved? Do you want to replace the covers?

What do you want to do to the walls and ceilings? Paper, paint, add texture, cladding, coving?

Home Office/Study

The keep/remove/replace/add checklist

	Keep	Remove	Replace	Add	Notes
Flooring					
Doors / Handles					
Window Covering					
Lighting					
Desk					
Chair					
Computer					
Printer					
Storage Cupboards					
TV					
Desk Lamp					
Desk Draws					
Rug					
Pictures					
Noticeboard					
Desk Organiser					
Sockets					

Home Office/Study

The keep/remove/replace/add checklist

	Keep	Remove	Replace	Add	Notes
Radiators					
Skirting Boards					

Home Office/Study

Plans & Drawings

Metres

Home Office/Study

Plans & Drawings

Metres

Home Office/Study

Buying list

Type:	Shop / Website
Description	
Cost	

Type:	Shop / Website
Description	
Cost	

Type:	Shop / Website
Description	
Cost	

Home Office/Study

Buying list

Type:	Shop / Website
Description	
Cost	

Type:	Shop / Website
Description	
Cost	

Type:	Shop / Website
Description	
Cost	

Home Office/Study

Buying list

Type:	Shop / Website
Description	
Cost	

Type:	Shop / Website
Description	
Cost	

Type:	Shop / Website
Description	
Cost	

Home Office/Study

Buying list

Type:	Shop / Website
Description	
Cost	

Type:	Shop / Website
Description	
Cost	

Type:	Shop / Website
Description	
Cost	

Total Buying List Cost for Room:

Home Office/Study
Budget

a) Room Budget

Item	Estimated Cost	Actual Cost
Preparation Costs		
Material Costs		
Buying List Costs		
Trades Costs		
Total		

b) Preparation Costs

Item	Estimated Cost	Actual Cost
Total		

Home Office/Study
Budget

c) Material Costs

Item	Estimated Cost	Actual Cost
Total		

d) Total Buying List Costs

Item	Estimated Cost	Actual Cost
Total		

Home Office/Study

Budget

e) Trades Cost

Type:	Trader's Name
Description of works:	
Quoted Cost:	Final Cost:

Type:	Trader's Name
Description of works:	
Quoted Cost:	Final Cost:

Type:	Trader's Name
Description of works:	
Quoted Cost:	Final Cost:

Total Trades Costs:

Overall Room Costs:

Home Office/Study

Time

Item	Estimated time	Key dates	Notes

Notes

Notes

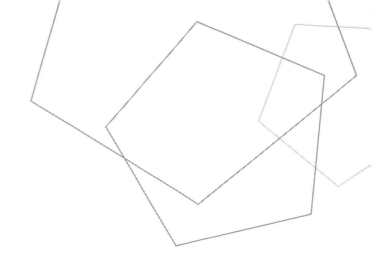

SPARE
PAGES

Room:_____

The questions

What do you like about the room as it is?

_____

_____

_____

_____

_____

What don't you like about the room as it is?

_____

_____

_____

_____

_____

How do you want to use it? How do you want it to feel?

_____

_____

_____

_____

_____

Room:_____

What design style are you going for in this room?

_____

_____

_____

_____

_____

What colours are you going to use?

_____

_____

_____

_____

_____

Are there any must haves in your room? Jot them down here.

_____

_____

_____

_____

_____

Room:_____

What sort of lighting do you want to have? LED ceiling lights, wall lights, standard lamps?

_____

_____

_____

_____

_____

Where are all the electrical sockets? Do they need to be moved?

_____

_____

_____

_____

_____

What do you want to do to the walls and ceilings? Paper, paint, add texture, cladding, coving?

_____

_____

_____

_____

_____

Room:_____

The questions

What do you like about the room as it is?

_____

_____

_____

_____

_____

What don't you like about the room as it is?

_____

_____

_____

_____

_____

How do you want to use it? How do you want it to feel?

_____

_____

_____

_____

_____

Room:_____

What design style are you going for in this room?

_____

_____

_____

_____

_____

What colours are you going to use?

_____

_____

_____

_____

_____

Are there any must haves in your room? Jot them down here.

_____

_____

_____

_____

_____

Room:_ _ _ _ _ _ _ _ _

What sort of lighting do you want to have? LED ceiling lights, wall lights, standard lamps?

Where are all the electrical sockets? Do they need to be moved?

What do you want to do to the walls and ceilings? Paper, paint, add texture, cladding, coving?

Room:_____

The questions

What do you like about the room as it is?

_____

_____

_____

_____

_____

What don't you like about the room as it is?

_____

_____

_____

_____

_____

How do you want to use it? How do you want it to feel?

_____

_____

_____

_____

_____

Room:_____

What design style are you going for in this room?

_____

_____

_____

_____

_____

What colours are you going to use?

_____

_____

_____

_____

_____

Are there any must haves in your room? Jot them down here.

_____

_____

_____

_____

_____

Room:_____

What sort of lighting do you want to have? LED ceiling lights, wall lights, standard lamps?

_____

_____

_____

_____

Where are all the electrical sockets? Do they need to be moved?

_____

_____

_____

_____

What do you want to do to the walls and ceilings? Paper, paint, add texture, cladding, coving?

_____

_____

_____

_____

Room_____

The keep/remove/replace/add checklist

	Keep	Remove	Replace	Add	Notes

Room_____

The keep/remove/replace/add checklist

	Keep	Remove	Replace	Add	Notes

Room_____

The keep/remove/replace/add checklist

	Keep	Remove	Replace	Add	Notes

Room_____

The keep/remove/replace/add checklist

	Keep	Remove	Replace	Add	Notes

Room_____

The keep/remove/replace/add checklist

	Keep	Remove	Replace	Add	Notes

Room_____

The keep/remove/replace/add checklist

	Keep	Remove	Replace	Add	Notes

Room:_____

Plans & Drawings

Metres

1   2   3   4   5

1   2   3   4   5

Room:_____

Plans & Drawings

Metres

1 2 3 4 5

1 2 3 4 5

Room:_____

Plans & Drawings

Metres

1   2   3   4   5

1   2   3   4   5

Room:_____

Plans & Drawings

Metres

1 2 3 4 5

1 2 3 4 5

Room:_____

Plans & Drawings

Metres

1 2 3 4 5

1 2 3 4 5

Room:_____

Plans & Drawings

Metres

Buying List

Type:	Shop / Website
Description	
Cost	

Type:	Shop / Website
Description	
Cost	

Type:	Shop / Website
Description	
Cost	

Buying List

Type:	Shop / Website
Description	
Cost	

Type:	Shop / Website
Description	
Cost	

Type:	Shop / Website
Description	
Cost	

Buying List

Type:	Shop / Website
Description	
Cost	

Type:	Shop / Website
Description	
Cost	

Type:	Shop / Website
Description	
Cost	

Buying List

Type:	Shop / Website
Description	
Cost	

Type:	Shop / Website
Description	
Cost	

Type:	Shop / Website
Description	
Cost	

Buying List

Type:	Shop / Website
Description	
Cost	

Type:	Shop / Website
Description	
Cost	

Type:	Shop / Website
Description	
Cost	

Buying List

Type:	Shop / Website
Description	
Cost	

Type:	Shop / Website
Description	
Cost	

Type:	Shop / Website
Description	
Cost	

Buying List

Type:	Shop / Website
Description	
Cost	

Type:	Shop / Website
Description	
Cost	

Type:	Shop / Website
Description	
Cost	

Buying List

Type:	Shop / Website
Description	
Cost	

Type:	Shop / Website
Description	
Cost	

Type:	Shop / Website
Description	
Cost	

Buying List

Type:	Shop / Website
Description	
Cost	

Type:	Shop / Website
Description	
Cost	

Type:	Shop / Website
Description	
Cost	

Buying List

Type:	Shop / Website
Description	
Cost	

Type:	Shop / Website
Description	
Cost	

Type:	Shop / Website
Description	
Cost	

Buying List

Type:	Shop / Website
Description	
Cost	

Type:	Shop / Website
Description	
Cost	

Type:	Shop / Website
Description	
Cost	

Buying List

Type:	Shop / Website

Description

Cost

Type:	Shop / Website

Description

Cost

Type:	Shop / Website

Description

Cost

_____ Budget

a) Room Budget

Item	Estimated Cost	Actual Cost
Preparation Costs		
Material Costs		
Buying List Costs		
Trades Costs		
Total		

b) Preparation Costs

Item	Estimated Cost	Actual Cost
Total		

_____ Budget

c) Material Costs

Item	Estimated Cost	Actual Cost
Total		

d) Total Buying List Costs

Item	Estimated Cost	Actual Cost
Total		

_____ Budget

e) Trades Cost

Type:	Trader's Name
Description of works:	
Quoted Cost:	**Final Cost:**

Type:	Trader's Name
Description of works:	
Quoted Cost:	**Final Cost:**

Type:	Trader's Name
Description of works:	
Quoted Cost:	**Final Cost:**

Total Trades Costs:

Overall Room Costs:

_____ Budget

a) Room Budget

Item	Estimated Cost	Actual Cost
Preparation Costs		
Material Costs		
Buying List Costs		
Trades Costs		
Total		

b) Preparation Costs

Item	Estimated Cost	Actual Cost
Total		

_____ Budget

c) Material Costs

Item	Estimated Cost	Actual Cost
Total		

d) Total Buying List Costs

Item	Estimated Cost	Actual Cost
Total		

_____ Budget

e) Trades Cost

Type:	Trader's Name
Description of works:	
Quoted Cost:	**Final Cost:**

Type:	Trader's Name
Description of works:	
Quoted Cost:	**Final Cost:**

Type:	Trader's Name
Description of works:	
Quoted Cost:	**Final Cost:**

Total Trades Costs:

Overall Room Costs:

_____ Budget

a) Room Budget

Item	Estimated Cost	Actual Cost
Preparation Costs		
Material Costs		
Buying List Costs		
Trades Costs		
Total		

b) Preparation Costs

Item	Estimated Cost	Actual Cost
Total		

_____ Budget

c) Material Costs

Item	Estimated Cost	Actual Cost
Total		

d) Total Buying List Costs

Item	Estimated Cost	Actual Cost
Total		

_____ Budget

e) Trades Cost

Type:	Trader's Name
Description of works:	
Quoted Cost:	**Final Cost:**

Type:	Trader's Name
Description of works:	
Quoted Cost:	**Final Cost:**

Type:	Trader's Name
Description of works:	
Quoted Cost:	**Final Cost:**

Total Trades Costs:

Overall Room Costs:

Room_____

Time

Item	Estimated time	Key dates	Notes

Room_____

Time

Item	Estimated time	Key dates	Notes

Room_____

Time

Item	Estimated time	Key dates	Notes

Notes

Notes

Notes

Notes

Notes

Notes

Printed in Great Britain
by Amazon

55414472R00124